Covenant and Kingdom

STUDY GUIDE

3DM Publishing

3dmpublishing.com

Covenant and Kingdom Guide

3dmpublishing.com

MichaelJamesBreen.com

Book quotes from *Covenant and Kingdom: The DNA of the Bible* by Mike Breen (3DM, 2010).

Printed in the United States of America

ISBN: 978-0-9990039-7-8

3DM Publishing

3dmpublishing.com

CONTENTS

About This Guide

Welcome to the study guide for *Covenant and Kingdom: The DNA of the Bible*.

WHY THIS GUIDE WAS CREATED

The Bible is meant to be read and understood. But many people struggle to interpret Scripture. I believe that Covenant and Kingdom offers the simplest framework of interpretation as we read the Bible for ourselves. These are the guiding coordinates, the latitude and longitude, that orient us as we read the Bible.

By understanding Covenant and Kingdom, we unlock the keys of interpretation that help us read the Bible for ourselves. While this approach cannot and should not replace in-depth Bible study, engaging the Bible through its largest themes remind us anew that the Bible is a book about God and us. This guide helps us begin to see and understand the double helix of Covenant and Kingdom that run throughout the Bible.

HOW THE QUESTIONS WORK

The questions and reflections you'll find in this guide are meant to evoke rather than inform. Let us explain. Too often, questions in guides like this end up being little more than thinly veiled attempts at content delivery. That isn't all bad. Information does help learning. But while question writers mean for people to explore the depths to which God is calling them, what often happens is that they can't resist "helping" a person come up with the "right" answer. And in doing so, these questions short-circuit people actually hearing the voice of God for themselves. While most people know this isn't the most effective way to learn, this style of questions persists because—if we are honest—many of us have our doubts that the Holy Spirit can do the Holy Spirit's job of leading each person into all truth. So we use leading questions in to fill the gap. It may be noble, but misguided.

This guide is trying to do something profoundly different. These questions are meant to evoke something. Jesus called that something the *kairos* (cf. Mark 1:15: "The *kairos* has come..."), that is, an opportunity to see God's kingdom, to turn aside and enter it through the doorway of your own heart. These questions are meant to help you help you and/or your group do two very basic biblical things: Repent and Believe.

First, these questions will give you a practical way to observe, reflect on, and discuss the things God is doing in your heart(s). In this process, thinking differently—repenting—becomes possible. Martin Luther said it this way: "When our Lord and Master Jesus Christ said, 'Repent,' he willed the entire life of believers to be one of repentance."

Second, this guide will seek to give you a practical way to plan, to act on what God has said, and to become accountable for following through. This process is about obeying Jesus' command in the Sermon on the Mount about the importance of actually doing what he said. Through this process, acting differently—believing—becomes possible.

Each section of this guide will go through these six steps:

- Observe
- Reflect
- Discuss
- Plan
- Account
- Act

If you're familiar with the Learning Circle, this will be familiar to you. If you're not familiar with it, you may want to check out *Building a Discipling Culture* or *Choosing to Learn from Life* by Mike Breen. But don't worry—this guide is structured in a way that will make sense to everyone, whether you're new to the Learning Circle or not.

Of course, if you are used to using the Learning Circle in a less formal manner, that's OK too. You can use the questions you'll find here as starters and let the conversation go from there.

The guide includes some key quotes from *Covenant and Kingdom* as a way to jog your memory and start your observations and reflection. Of course, you are welcome to include any thoughts or passages from the book or from Scripture in your discussion.

The questions in this guide will start out differently in each section, but the questions about the Account and Act steps will be virtually the same every time. This is intentional, because the goal of this guide is not to lead you to act in a certain way—it's to encourage and empower you to act in the way God is specifically leading you. Rather than suggesting potential plans of action, this guide will trust you to listen to the leading of the Holy Spirit with your particular *kairos*. This means that groups may have vastly different plans in any given week. That's OK—it's a sign that the Holy Spirit is actively working in your group in dynamically powerful ways.

Of course, the way that these questions work will be different depending on whether you choose to use it individually or in a group. But whether you use this guide to supplement your personal study, or in a group of people who are learning to study the Bible together, the format will work either way. One note here—if you are doing this individually, you still may choose to discuss what you're learning and what your plans to act are with a friend, a spouse, or a mentor. That's because actually discussing these things will make you more likely to actually be accountable to act. So try to find a way to do that.

A few more thoughts about questions:

- Questions are doorways. Walk through the doorway they open. Jesus used questions as a way of opening people's hearts.
- Questions are meant to start conversations, not end them. See what the question uncovers and where the Holy Spirit is leading.
- Questions require space. Often you'll need time to process before responding. In that vein, silence is golden. Don't rush through the questions, either on your own or in a group context.

THE SECTIONS OF THIS GUIDE

You'll want to use this guide in conjunction with the *Covenant and Kingdom* book, because it is divided based on sections of that book.

The 12 sections (with page numbers) are:

1. Basics of Covenant and Kingdom: Introduction (ix to xvii)
2. Creation and the Fall: Chapters 1-2 (1-16)
3. Abraham: Man of Covenant: Chapter 3 (17-38)
4. Joseph: Man of Kingdom: Chapter 4 (39-64)
5. Moses: Priest and Prince: Chapter 5 (65-94)
6. David: Worshipper and Warrior: Chapter 6 (95-120)
7. Connecting the Old and New Testaments: Chapter 7 (121-134)
8. Jesus: Son of God and Son of Man: Chapters 8-10 (135-158)
9. Jesus' Ministry: Chapters 11-12 (159-180)
10. Journey to the Cross: Chapters 13-14 (181-200)
11. The Message Spreads: Chapters 15-16 (201-230)
12. Tools for Interpretation: Chapter 17 (231-251)

If you are doing this guide as individual study, you'll want to read a section of that book before starting the questions, and then keep the book open as you use them. If you're doing this guide in a group, at least the leader will need to have a copy of the book at hand. Of course, any group member will benefit from using the book in conjunction with this guide.

A BLESSING AS YOU BEGIN

As you use this guide,
May your passion to study the Bible be rekindled
And may you discover more than ever
That you are held in the hands of another.

SECTION 1

Basics of Covenant and Kingdom

COVENANT AND KINGDOM
INTRODUCTION
PAGES IX–XVII

KEY QUOTES

Introduction

Covenant and Kingdom is one of the simplest frameworks for interpreting the Bible as we read the Bible for ourselves.

page xiii

Covenant is the way in which the Bible describes and defines relationship: first our relationship with God and then our relationship with everyone else.

page xv

Kingdom is the way in which the Bible describes and defines responsibility: first our responsibility to represent God to the people we know and then to everyone else.

page xvi

OBSERVE Do you ever struggle to read the Bible? When does this commonly happen?

REFLECT Do you ever struggle to understand the Bible? Why do you think that happens?

Think about a time when the Bible came alive to you.

- What specifically came alive?
- Why do you think it came alive?
- How long did this breakthrough last?

DISCUSS Have you ever thought about Covenant and Kingdom as the DNA of the Bible?

- What are some other ways or terms you can use to describe the theme of Covenant?
- What are some other ways or terms you can use to describe the theme of Kingdom?

PLAN How might God be leading you to engage the Bible differently than you currently are?

ACCOUNT How will you record what God is calling you to do? How will you share your plan with someone else?

ACT How did you follow through on your plan?

SECTION 2

Creation and the Fall

COVENANT AND KINGDOM
CHAPTERS 1–2
PAGES 1–16

KEY QUOTES

CHAPTER 1

Creation

God intended that people would bear his imprint, and even rule the world. They would reflect his identity and represent him to all of creation. Even the angelic court of heaven was to be secondary to God's purposes in this. Humankind would be his sole representatives on the earth. They and they alone would be the means by which God would govern the earth.

page 3

Freedom of choice was given as a sign of their relationship when God made them. He wanted them to choose partnership (being one with him), but they chose independence, self-determination and separation. Human beings continue to make this choice. But the consequence of this decision was not only separation from God. The consequence was even more serious. Because the connection to Life was severed, Adam and Eve began to die. And their broken relationship meant that they also surrendered their capacity to rule. In submitting to the temptation of the serpent, Adam and Eve lost their rightful place before God and surrendered their throne—making room for the accession of another, would be later be known as the devil.

page 8

CHAPTER 2

After the Fall

God is drawn toward us by his great love but simultaneously repelled by the ugliness of our sin. Incredibly, though, God's love is greater than his judgment—his impulse to embrace is greater than his impulse to reject.

page 13

Since we had lost our close relationship with God, our relationships with one another were always susceptible to division. God wanted to build a secure foundation for the unity of humankind, and he would do this by creating a Covenant relationship with us. By making a Covenant and "being one" with us, he would enable us to "be one" with each other.

page 16

OBSERVE

Where do you find the theme of Covenant in the story of creation? Where do you find the theme of Kingdom in the story of creation?

How did the fall affect our Covenant relationship with God? How did the fall affect our Kingdom responsibility from God?

REFLECT

Why is it significant that our Covenant relationship with God begins with the way he created us? Why is it significant that our Kingdom responsibility from God begins with his actions at Creation?

When you view the fall through the themes of Covenant and Kingdom, how do you see the fall differently? What new insights into the fall and our falleness as humans do these themes illuminate?

How do Covenant and Kingdom help us understand the way God set about to restore the world after the fall?

DISCUSS

Consider how the themes of Covenant and Kingdom bring you new understanding of these Bible stories:

- The flood (Genesis 6-9)
- The tower of Babel (Genesis 11)

PLAN

How will you read the first chapters of Genesis with the themes of Covenant and Kingdom in mind?

How will you record the *kairos* you gain as you read?

ACCOUNT

How will you record what God is calling you to do? How will you share your plan with someone else?

ACT

How did you follow through on your plan?

SECTION 3

Abraham: Man of Covenant

COVENANT AND KINGDOM
CHAPTER 3
PAGES 17–38

KEY QUOTES

CHAPTER 3

Abraham: Man of Covenant

The Lord offered himself as Abram's protection (shield) and provision (reward). Abram could rest in the confidence that he was protected and provided for. But there was much more than this hidden in God's promise to Abram. "Shield" and "sovereign" are the same word in Hebrew. By using this word, the Lord pointed to himself as the King of heaven, offering to bless Abram with a royal blessing.

page 22

Abram chose to believe God. In Abram's world, only the words of a Covenant partner could truly be trusted. However, Abram chose to trust God's words as if they were spoken by a Covenant partner. And so God related to Abram in exactly the same way.

page 23

God gave Abram "righteousness"—or a "right relationship" where no "wrong" could spoil it. This had to be given by God as a gift—Abram could not have it by any right or effort of his own. God had extended an invitation to Abram: an invitation to a journey that would lead all the way back to the Garden of Eden.

page 24

The Lord's presence, like fire, both attracts and repels. We draw near for warmth but must keep our distance, lest we be burned. God's love draws us toward him, but his holiness threatens to consume us as we come closer. In the end, it is our decision how close we come and how willing we are to risk being consumed.

page 25

The Lord took the initiative, but Abram was a willing participant, and the result was true "at-one-ment." Atonement means precisely what the word suggests. A Covenant sacrifice means that we "become one" with God. Because they had "cut a Covenant," the greater and stronger partner (the Lord) had conferred upon the lesser and weaker partners (Abram and Sarai) the right to be equal partners with him. Covenants with God always depend on the initiative of his grace.

page 27

There is another vital component in a Covenant relationship, which is submission. This is described most commonly in Scripture as obedience.

page 33

In our walk with God, our capacity for perseverance in difficulties, and the ability to obey will be determined by how secure we feel in our relationship with him. If we begin with our new identity, given to us in the Covenant we share with God, then we will have security; security will lead to confidence, and confidence to courage.

page 35

OBSERVE

What did you learn about Covenant when you studied this chapter and the corresponding Scripture?

- From the cutting of Covenant (Genesis 15)
- From the new names (Genesis 17)
- From the call to sacrifice (Genesis 22)

REFLECT

What did Abram do that reflected he understood what it meant to be God's Covenant partner? What did Abram do that showed he didn't fully understand this identity?

Why does our identity as God's Covenant partner naturally lead to obedience?

What are some reasons we fail to embrace our identity as God's children? What are some reasons we fail to obey God as our Covenant Father? What are some reasons that we fail to talk to God the way Abram did?

DISCUSS

Consider the practical outgrowths of our Covenant relationship with God, and discuss whether you are living as God's Covenant partner. Use these questions to prompt this discussion:

- What words are you longing to hear from God that would make your heart leap?
- Look into Jesus' face: Is there a look of disappointment toward you, or a smile?
- In what ways has God confirmed his relationship with you, assuring you that he is near you? In what ways would you like him to do this?
- Do you believe that God says about you what God says about Jesus: You are my beloved son; I am very pleased in you? Why or why not?
- What identity have you been holding onto that you need to let go of in order to embrace your identity as God's dearly loved son or daughter?
- What barriers do you have to surrendering your life to God's? Can you give them up right now?

PLAN How are you going to start:

- Embracing a new part of your Covenant relationship with God
- Submitting to God through increased obedience
- Talking to God as a Covenant partner
- Or taking some other step toward God through his Covenant with you?

ACCOUNT How will you record what God is calling you to do? How will you share your plan with someone else?

ACT How did you follow through on your plan?

SECTION 4

Joseph: Man of Kingdom

COVENANT AND KINGDOM
CHAPTER 4
PAGES 39–64

KEY QUOTES

CHAPTER 4

Joseph: Called to Kingdom Rule

Being the "ruler" over Egypt was the unmistakable calling of Joseph's life. He was called to take on a role that God had prepared for him. Joseph's relationship to Pharaoh was symbolic of his (and our) relationship with God. There was, of course, only one King, but he chose to rule "through" Joseph. He was to become the governor of the greatest nation on the earth, and in this, he was likewise the empowered emissary of God in the world.

page 43

God's presence caused Joseph to prosper. Despite Joseph's faults and these terrible circumstances, God proved faithful to his Covenant promise of provision and protection.

page 47

Here is the Kingdom paradox: victory comes only when we surrender to the One who brings true Victory.

page 49

Only when God is at the center of our lives can he work through us in the way he intends to. God wants to rule through us, with divine authority and power, but to do this, he must know that he is on the throne of our hearts.

page 51

For God's Kingdom to be revealed, we need to move beyond our merely human aspirations. So if the distinction is to be made, what is required? The answer is expressed in the life of Joseph and more perfectly portrayed in the life of Christ. There needs to be both death and resurrection. Our feelings of self-importance, and our belief that we are the "center of the universe," have to die, so that God can be enthroned as the King of our circumstances and his vision for our life can live.

pages 58-9

Genuine Kingdom breakthrough is seen only through personal brokenness. Only God—the King of Heaven—can reveal the Kingdom of heaven here on earth.

page 59

(The Lord) wants to express his Kingdom and extend his rule through us. His eyes are forever casting about the earth, looking for hearts that are prepared and ready—surrendered, choosing the path of obedience. And when he finds those hearts? Then the Kingdom pours through, because the Lord has found the channel through which he can release his blessing.

page 61

OBSERVE

What did it take for Joseph to surrender and move out of the center of his own world? What did this surrender look like practically?

Did Joseph have a spirit of poverty or abundance when he looked at his Covenant partner? Which kind of spirit do you tend to have?

REFLECT

What kept Joseph from fully expressing his Kingdom responsibility earlier in his life? How have you faced this same obstacle in your life?

DISCUSS

What does surrender look like in your real life and your current circumstances?

What would it look like for you to actually move out of the center of your own life?

Where or when have you despised your Kingdom gifts or felt the need to cover them up? Why did this happen?

Where have you seen your personal brokenness and/or surrender lead to Kingdom breakthrough? What did that Kingdom breakthrough look like?

How do we learn to see our brokenness as a doorway to Kingdom breakthrough? What keeps us from doing this?

PLAN

Consider whether your *kairos* is leading you to answer one of these two questions:

1. What is one step of surrender God is calling you to take?
2. Or, what is one area of brokenness God is calling you to engage?

How will you begin to do this?

ACCOUNT

How will you record what God is calling you to do? How will you share your plan with someone else?

ACT How did you follow through on your plan?

SECTION 5

Moses: Priest and Prince

COVENANT AND KINGDOM
CHAPTER 5
PAGES 65–94

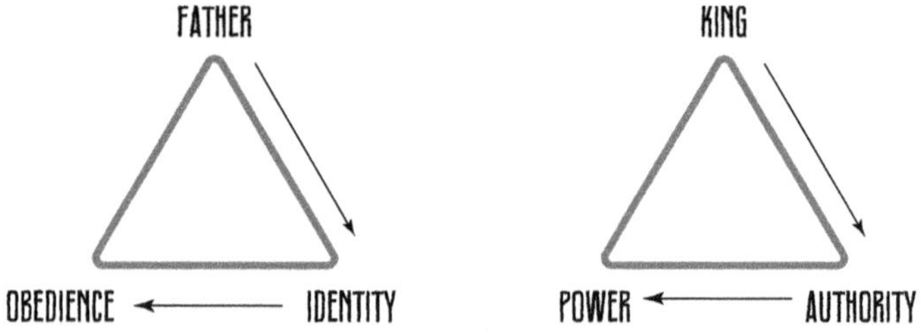

KEY QUOTES

CHAPTER 5

Moses: Priest and Prince

In the life of Moses (and later in David), we can see what happens when Covenant and Kingdom combine.

page 67

The Lord had come to reveal himself "in flames of fire." Fire burns and repels. The Lord is transcendent—holy, mysterious and unapproachable. Fire warms, too, and it attracts. The Lord is immanent—present, involved and responsive. Fire is the symbol of God's presence.

page 71

When someone is sure in his identity, he tends to live out a certain measure of self-confidence.

page 72

Identity is always given from the outside before it becomes reality on the inside. Moses heard God confirm his identity. In time, his confidence grew, and his long-dormant capacity to lead emerged.

page 74

This pattern of building, breaking and blessing is seen in all of the great characters of biblical history. God wants to use us, but we are not fully usable until we have surrendered ourselves completely into his hands.

page 76

The Lord wanted Moses to take responsibility for his calling. But God wanted Moses to receive that responsibility with the confidence that comes from a deep and loving relationship. The Lord had come "in fire" to Moses—but not to destroy him. God's burning presence had come to consume the bonds that bound Moses' heart. As Moses received his calling and heard the Lord set out his destiny, the chains of failure and insecurity fell away. And as Moses took his first faltering steps toward true freedom, his spirit, long bowed down by years of guilt and separation, began to wake up and respond to the call. Free at last! Now he could bring freedom to his people. Only those who are free can set others free.

page 79

Each of the ten plagues underlined the superiority of the Kingdom of God over the kingdom of darkness. The Egyptian pantheon was exposed for what it was: a pale and futile imitation of the Creator's power.

page 81

If we try to relate to God through obedience first, we will always be striving for his approval, immobilized by constant insecurity. We will be held away from God rather to him. Our good works and best intentions can never be good enough to pave the way toward a holy God, and the struggle to obey will in itself lead to separation.

page 88

OBSERVE

Think through the major events of Moses' life. How do you see the themes of Covenant and/or Kingdom in these events:

- His birth and early life (Exodus 1-2)
- The burning bush (Exodus 3-4)
- The clash with Pharaoh (Exodus 5-11)
- The Passover (Exodus 12)
- The escape from Egypt (Exodus 13-14)
- The giving of the law (Exodus 19-20)

REFLECT

What kept Moses from initially embracing his Covenant identity and living out his Kingdom responsibility? Which of these obstacles were internal, and which were external? How did Moses move past these obstacles?

How did God publicly confirm Moses' Covenant identity and Kingdom responsibility? How does God do this in our lives?

DISCUSS

Do you primarily see God as Father or King? Why?

- Looking at the Covenant triangle, how do you currently see God—as a Father who demands obedience or a Father who gives identity?
- Looking at the Kingdom triangle, how do you currently see God—as a King who abuses power or a King who gives authority?

Is Covenant or Kingdom more difficult for you to live into? Why?

PLAN

Consider whether your *kairos* is leading you to one of these two areas:

- What desert may God be leading you into? Why might the brokenness of the desert be necessary? Why is brokenness a necessary prelude to surrender?
- What bold Kingdom calling may God be calling you to embrace? Why does this calling seem difficult or even impossible? How might God help you take embrace this calling like he helped Moses?

ACCOUNT

How will you record what God is leading you to do? How will you share your plan with someone else?

ACT

How did you follow through on your plan?

SECTION 6

David: Worshipper and Warrior

COVENANT AND KINGDOM
CHAPTER 6
PAGES 95–120

KEY QUOTES

CHAPTER 6

David: Worshipper and Warrior

David's heart was fashioned in the light of a Covenant relationship with the Lord. This was the rich resource in David's songwriting and the solid foundation on which he built a life of purpose. The security that came from his walk with God bred first confidence and then an incredible courage as David sought to extend the Lord's kingly rule.

page 104

Do we have the Covenant confidence that David showed, as we face the giants in our lives? Are we able to stand on the security God gives us, or do we cower among the crowd, hoping for others to wear someone else's armor? When we look to anyone other than God for our protection, we may find safety in the short term, but our confidence to stand never grows.

page 108

Saul never fully surrendered his heart to God, and so never knew the confidence I the Lord that David enjoyed. From Saul's high position on the throne of Israel, he had no competitors; and yet to the king, David felt like a threat. But in attacking David, Saul had lifted his hand against the Lord. And though the path was long and at times torturous for David, the conclusion was assured: Saul was certain to lose the throne, and David would be given Saul's kingdom.

page 111

What David revealed in his life was that even though God makes a Covenant promise, we still have to engage in Kingdom warfare to possess the promise. God had promised the land of Israel to Abraham, and although Joshua and Caleb had led and fought well, at the end of their lives, the job remained incomplete. It needed David's total determination to secure final possession of what had been promised.

page 114

David's deep faith in God meant that David did not try to make things happen for himself. Confidence in God's promises meant that David had waited for God to do things in his time.

page 117

Worship was David's intimate expression of Covenant relationship—the connecting of his heart to God. Warfare, on the other hand, was the ultimate expression of Kingdom authority and power, resulting in David taking possession of what God had promised.

page 118

Kingdom courage flows from Covenant confidence.

page 120

OBSERVE

Think through the major events of David's life. How do you see the themes of Covenant and/or Kingdom in these events:

- His anointing (1 Samuel 16)
- His worship (Psalm 23 and many others)
- His battle with Goliath (1 Samuel 17)
- His Covenant friendship with Jonathan (1 Samuel 18)
- His reign as king (2 Samuel 1-5)
- His desire to build the temple (2 Samuel 7)

REFLECT

Which came first for David—knowledge of his Covenant identity or his Kingdom calling? Why did God do things in that order?

David had a long season of waiting before beginning his fight for God's Kingdom? Have you had a similar wait? What did you learn from it?

DISCUSS

What specific differences did you observe between Saul's life as king and David's life as king? What can we learn from these differences?

The book makes the connection between the battles David fought and the battles Jesus fought (page 114-5). What battles did Jesus fight when he was on earth? What do these battles teach us about his Kingdom? How do these battles help us understand our Kingdom responsibility better?

Why does God want us to fight for his Kingdom? How does this fight make us feel? When and how do we try to avoid it?

PLAN

Consider whether your *kairos* is leading you to answer one of these two questions:

- What step of worship is God calling you to embrace?
- What step of warfare is God calling you to embrace?

ACCOUNT

How will you record what God is leading you to do? How will you share your plan with someone else?

ACT How did you follow through on your plan?

SECTION 7

Connecting the Old and New Testaments

COVENANT AND KINGDOM
CHAPTER 7
PAGES 121–134

KEY QUOTES

The Journey So Far

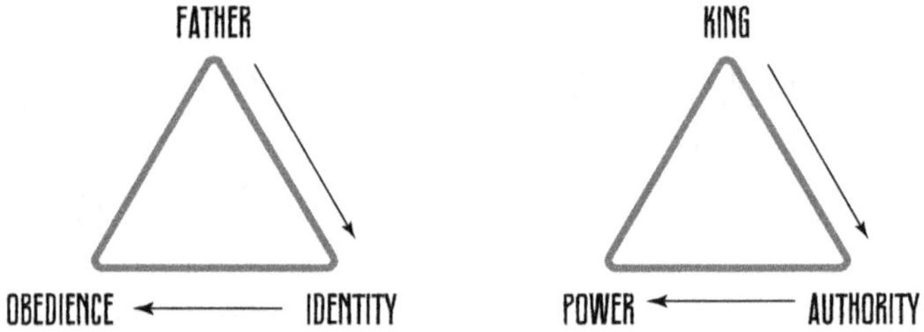

Power is exercised as a direct result of having authority. The nature of this power requires a level of personal surrender that prevents people being the object of others' praise.... Power always flows from authority. Authority is about placing ourselves in the right place before God. As we humbly recognize his and our position, he authorizes us to exercise power on his behalf.

page 128

CHAPTER 7

Connecting the Old and New Testaments

The kings of the divided kingdom began first to walk and then to run away from God. Without a Covenant relationship, they had progressively less authority to represent God as the king. There were a few notable exceptions, such as King Josiah of Judah, but in general, the Kingship of God was no longer represented by men who knew him. Things went from bad to worse.

page 131

They knew that the Lord had rescued them and had set things right before. They knew that he had promised through the prophets that one like David would come and establish an everlasting Kingdom. But when would it happen?

page 133

OBSERVE How did God's people lose their way? What were the results in terms of God's Kingdom?

REFLECT This section of the book describes how God's Covenant love persisted even when God's people did not live out their identity. When have you found your life in a similar pattern?

This section of the book also describes the deep longing God's people had to escape the circumstances of peril and live in God's Kingdom as God intended. When have you felt a similar longing?

DISCUSS Why do we not live the way God intends in terms of Covenant identity?

Why do we not live the way God intends in terms of Kingdom calling?

PLAN What *kairos* has God brought to mind as you reflected

on the end of the Old Testament and the period between the testaments? What plan will you undertake to respond to this *kairos*?

ACCOUNT How will you record what God is leading you to do? How will you share your plan with someone else?

ACT How did you follow through on your plan?

SECTION 8

Jesus: Son of God and Son of Man

COVENANT AND KINGDOM
CHAPTERS 8–10
PAGES 135–158

KEY QUOTES

CHAPTER 8

Jesus: Son of God and Son of Man

These two great themes of the Bible find their fullest expression in Jesus. Only when we look at him are we able to grasp their complete meaning. For example, in the Gospels, Jesus is given many titles, but perhaps the two most important are Son of God and Son of Man.

page 137

On the Cross, Jesus reconnected the Kingdom of heaven with the people of earth. On the Cross, God stretched wide his arms to embrace us all. Kingdom and Covenant are writ large. The banner headline above Jesus' head proclaimed that he was the King and the blood that flowed from his wounds indicated the sacrifice necessary to make a Covenant possible. As the vertical and horizontal bars of the Cross were bound together to form an instrument of execution and torture, so both threads of Scripture were captured in time. The vast sweep of the story of God and the immeasurable depth of his love found their focus here, definitively expressed.

page 139

When we understand who Jesus was and what he did, we understand fully who we can be and what he calls us to do.

page 140

CHAPTER 9

Jesus' Baptism

John the Baptist strode onto the stage of history as "a voice of one calling in the desert." His message was simple: God wanted a relationship with his people again. If they would only return to their Covenant, they would be prepared to welcome Israel's new King. One like David was coming, and he would defeat their enemies, give them peace and establish a Kingdom that would never end. The baptism John offered symbolized the washing away of the sins that separated the people from God. But there was a less obvious present, too: the voluntary giving up of one life to receive another. Being immersed below the waters was like death, and reemerging was embracing the new life of a Covenant relationship with God.

page 143

The heavens were rent and the two worlds were connected as the Holy Spirit descended and remained on Jesus. The Holy Spirit had connected this world with the world to come as in that moment Jesus became the portal of the Kingdom of heaven. He was identified as the perfect representation of God's kingly authority and power. From this point on, wherever Jesus was found, the King was present. All that was present in heaven was no available through him—forgiveness for sin, healing for sickness, deliverance from demonic bondage, freedom from all captivity such as the stultifying effects of poverty and injustice… Jesus was established as the conduit of God's Kingship on earth. Anyone who came to Jesus would be able to receive the everlasting life of the Kingdom because it was flowing through him.

page 145

In submitting to baptism, Jesus was offering to represent us in the Covenant exchange. He was prepared to embrace the estranged condition and its full consequence of death. He would walk the path of death, fully identifying with us. He would give up his life so that we could live.

page 146

Our life of discipleship begins in Covenant and Kingdom of which baptism is the first sign. Thereafter, we should expect that the heavens are open above us and that the Kingship of God flows through our lives. And we should live in the full confidence that we are sons and daughters of the King whom we know intimately as Father.

page 147

CHAPTER 10

Tempted in the Desert

There appears to be a connection between the temptations Jesus resisted in the desert and the power he later exercised. For Jesus to exercise the power of the Kingdom, he needed the authority of the King. This was established when the Father stated clearly that Jesus was his Son. Jesus' identity and therefore his authority to wield heavenly power were established in his baptism. Jesus was the heir to heaven's throne, and so all the authority and power of God were resident within the Son.

page 153

(The devil) will seek to undermine our identity as children of God. Just as Jesus, we need to use the truth of God's word, which tells us that we are children of God.

page 156

OBSERVE

Think through the early events of Jesus' life. How do you see the truths of Covenant and/or Kingdom in:

- Jesus' miraculous birth
- Jesus' baptism
- Jesus' temptation

REFLECT

What new insights about Jesus' Covenant identity did you find as you read about Jesus' early life with new eyes? What new insight about Jesus' Kingship did you find?

What are the things that keep you from fully surrendering to God as Jesus did?

DISCUSS

How would Jesus answer the question: Who are you? How would you answer that question?

Did Jesus earn his identity, or was it given to him? Is yours earned or given?

What are reactions have you seen (or had) when a person's identity is threatened?

Recognizing that all of us are tempted, which of the devil's temptations trips you up the most:

- Appetite
- Ambition
- Affirmation

PLAN

What disciplines of disengagement do you need to help you say no to temptation?

Who knows you and will hold you accountable to your plan?

ACCOUNT

How will you record what God is leading you to do? How will you share your plan with someone else?

ACT

How did you follow through on your plan?

SECTION 9

Jesus' Ministry

COVENANT AND KINGDOM
CHAPTERS 11–12
PAGES 159–180

KEY QUOTES

CHAPTER 11

Jesus' Ministry Begins

When Jesus turned the water into wine, he was showing that he was taking all of the "Old" and making something deeper, richer, and much more satisfying in the "New." Although the "New" would contain all the elements of the "Old," it would be far better.

page 161

Jesus' incredible authority, amazing power and relentless determination were thoroughly captivating, and people hung on his every word. Through him, all the power of the Kingdom of heaven poured out and touched those he encountered. All that humanity longed for in heaven was revealed on earth in Jesus.

page 163

If they wanted to live the new life of the New Covenant on offer in him, they would have to live according to the terms that he offered. They would have to take him into their lives. If they did, then their souls would be nourished, and they would live forever.

pages 165-166

In the New Covenant, we "become one" with Jesus. We take him into ourselves as we would take in food. Covenant is about sharing identity. In the New Covenant, Jesus becomes part of us—fully integrated into the fabric of our being.

page 167

We have already seen that the New Covenant means that we are one with Jesus. Therefore, we must have the same message and ministry as him! His challenge to us is to reveal God's future in our lives. We are to declare that the "King is among us," and we are to heal the sick, deliver the oppressed, cleanse the alienated and even raise the dead!

page 167

CHAPTER 12

Retreat and Revelation

Peter declared that Jesus was both the long-awaited Messiah and the Son of God who gave all things life. "Messiah" represented the King, and the "Son" related to the Father. Representation and relationship—Kingdom and Covenant—intersected in Peter's first "confession."

page 173

Essentially, Peter was given one of Jesus' names—they had "become one" in Covenant. By implication, this also meant that Peter and Jesus shared the same identity. Therefore, Peter had all the benefits of a Covenant connection with the one from whom Jesus derived his identity—God the Father. Jesus as the Son of God was sharing his identity, and that meant Peter was part of the family.

pages 174-175

Similar to Peter, all Christians have a Covenant with Jesus. We all share his identity and carry his name.

*page 175*We have seen in the early ministry of Jesus in Capernaum and Galilee that invitation and challenge were deeply embedded in the way he related to his disciples. Jesus gave an invitation to Covenant relationship and a challenge to take responsibility for Kingdom representation.

page 177

When we observe the patterns of behavior Jesus took toward his followers, we see him constantly calibrating invitation and challenge to draw them on in their discipleship. Invitation and challenge were the two constants. If it was the crowd who knew little of him, then Jesus offered both invitation and challenge at a lower level to that which he shared with his closest followers. We can expect the Lord to do the same with us. By his Spirit, he continues to disciple his followers in the same way that he always has. He invites us to share deeply in a relationship of love with him. But at the same time, he challenges us to represent him in ever-widening spheres of influence.

page 178

OBSERVE

How did Peter model what it looks like to join God in a Covenant relationship? How did Peter model what it looks like to embrace God-given Kingdom responsibility?

Where did Peter thrive? Where did Peter struggle? What can we learn from his successes and failures?

REFLECT

How did Jesus calibrate invitation and challenge?

- Who got more invitation? Who got less invitation?
- Who got more challenge? Who got less challenge?
- When did invitation tend to come? When did challenge tend to come?

DISCUSS

What does it mean to "become one" with Jesus? What do we have to surrender? What do we gain?

What works of Kingdom power can we expect God to do through us? Does your picture of this tend to be too big or too small? Why do you think that is?

Where is Jesus reaching out to you with invitation right now? Where is Jesus speaking to you with challenge right now?

PLAN

What *kairos* has God brought to mind as you reflected on invitation and challenge in Jesus' ministry? How will you plan to respond to this *kairos* and to Jesus' invitation and/or challenge?

ACCOUNT

How will you record what God is leading you to do? How will you share your plan with someone else?

ACT

How did you follow through on your plan?

SECTION 10

Journey to the Cross

COVENANT AND KINGDOM
CHAPTERS 13–14
PAGES 181–200

KEY QUOTES

CHAPTER 13

Journey to Jerusalem and the Cross

The most important celebration of Israel's Covenant with God was gathered up by Jesus into the New Covenant in him. It was a Covenant that would be established in his death and sealed with his blood. The blood of Passover daubed on the doors of the Israelites meant that they could go into freedom, having been rescued from death. The blood of Jesus means that we are released from the prospect of spiritual death because he died in our place. And now we walk free because of his sacrifice.

page 184

Jesus took our place and walked the pathway of blood on our behalf. He had once traveled a pathway of blood at his own birth, passing from one side of the Covenant exchange to the other. In his death, he traveled the pathway back to reconnect us with God. He was born as one of us and died on behalf of us all.

page 186

Because of his sacrifice, and our Covenant relationship with our Father, we can have Covenant relationships with each other.

page 186

In the same way that the blessings of the Kingdom were poured through Jesus in his life, so the "Last Battle" and the Day of Judgment were revealed in his death.

page 187

CHAPTER 14

The Story of Jesus Continues: What Happened Next?

The open grave was no longer a fear-filled sign of death. It was now an invitation to a new life. As the portal to the coming Kingdom, even his dead body could not hold back the future blessings that God had stored up. Though his body was dead, life came to his body and raised him up.

page 195

All who have received Jesus, and therefore his Holy Spirit, are marked by the presence of the Spirit. When we receive Jesus, the Holy Spirit becomes a permanent presence in our life—as though our hearts were scarred. Jesus took his place on the throne his Father had prepared for his Son. Jesus wears the Crown of Kingship, and he bears the marks of Covenant. Incredibly, humanity has been admitted into the Godhead, and in Jesus, we sat down in heaven.

page 196

Through the death of Jesus, a Covenant had been made that gave the opportunity for humanity to be restored to its original place. God's intention had always been to win human beings back to himself and fill them with his presence so that the void in their life, created when they pulled away from him, could be filled again. As the Holy Spirit filled the disciples, his presence and power remade the connection, and he began the process of personal transformation. As we come to Christ, all of us receive the Holy Spirit who does the same for us. He connects us to our Creator and begins remaking us in his image.

page 198

OBSERVE

How is the Cross a story of substitutionary death? How is the Cross a story of victory over death and God's enemies?

What does substitution mean for identity, specifically for your efforts to earn God's love or prove yourself?

What gets set free in the human heart when you realize judgment day has already come? What gets set free for you specifically?

How does Jesus' victory on the Cross speak to failure, specifically to your failures?

How is Pentecost a story of Covenant? How is it a story of Kingdom?

REFLECT

How does the Passover prefigure the Covenant and Kingdom themes we later find on the Cross? What does this tell us about God's Covenant relationship and Kingdom plans across time?

How does the Cross teach us about the Day of Judgment to come? How will the Kingdom defeat its enemies in the end?

Read 1 Corinthians 15:54-57 as a prayer of celebration of this victory.

DISCUSS

How does Jesus' substitutionary sacrifice on the Cross unlock our Covenant relationship with God? How does it unlock our Covenant relationships with each other? Why do you think God made this part of our Covenant gift?

In the sidebar on the Lord's Prayer, the book says: The Covenant gives us great confidence as we ask, but the

Kingdom is not yet fully revealed. (page 191) How do you face this tension as you pray?

PLAN

How is God calling you to respond to:

- His subsitutionary sacrifice
- His Kingdom victory on the Cross

What *kairos* are these truths awakening in your heart?

ACCOUNT

How will you record what God is leading you to do? How will you share your plan with someone else?

ACT

How did you follow through on your plan?

SECTION 11

The Message Spreads

COVENANT AND KINGDOM
CHAPTERS 15–16
PAGES 201–230

KEY QUOTES

CHAPTER 15

The Story of Jesus Continues: The Message Spreads

We see the Covenant community of disciples functioning with the same Kingdom authority and power seen in Jesus' life.

page 203

The Sanhedrin were amazed at Peter and John's courage: how could such men as these speak and act with such authority? The answer was simple. They had been discipled by Jesus. They understood that their identity was bound up with that of their Lord. They were men who had a living Covenant relationship with God. They knew who they were, and knew that they were authorized to act on his behalf. They knew deep within that they carried the authority and power of the King.

page 204

The Lord was so connected to his followers through the New Covenant that when they were hurt by persecutors such as Saul felt it. This revelation later became the basis of Paul's theology of the church—he went on to describe it as "the body of Christ."

page 206

Paul contended that the Holy Spirit within the churches was the permanent mark of a new Covenant relationship with God. Paul encouraged people to be "filled with the Spirit," to "walk with the Spirit," to demonstrate the "fruit of the Spirit" in their lives and to live by his "power" daily.

page 209

CHAPTER 16

The Story Nears its Fulfillment

Even though the power of God expressed in the life of Paul was already functioning at a remarkable level, he would discover how surrender would give him access to even more. The many difficulties and persecutions that he suffered at the hands of those whom he probably described as his "thorns in the flesh" were the way in which God brought Paul to a fresh level of submission and an extraordinary experience of God's power.

page 216

It seems as though Paul's submission to God allowed the Lord to use him to release even greater levels of Kingdom power.

page 217

Jesus had given Paul a gracious invitation to live in a Covenant relationship with the Son of God. Even though Paul had brutally persecuted Jesus' followers, Jesus loved Paul. Such grace had overwhelmed Paul. Grace became the central message of his life.

page 218

Even though the early churches were mercilessly persecuted, the compelling life of their community and the power at work among them drew many into a relationship with God.

page 222

The Covenant people of God will see the Kingdom win through and the rule of darkness will be vanished. Between now and then, we are encouraged to see things from God's perspective and realize that his plans will come to their fulfillment with the triumphant return of Christ. The New Testament closes on a triumphant note with the promise of a returning King. When all the battles are fought and won, our King Jesus will return and gather his Covenant community to himself. Then heaven and earth will be remade, and the New Creation revealed.

pages 222-223

OBSERVE

How do we see Covenant and Kingdom at work in the way that the early church lived—for example, in the way Peter and John spoke to the Sanhedrin?

How do we see oneness between God and his Covenant people in the way he responds to Saul's persecution?

REFLECT

How is the Holy Spirit a proper sign of the Covenant carried by God's people?

How did Paul's surrender unlock even greater Kingdom breakthrough in his life?

What are the barriers that we need to remove that keep us from experiencing Jesus?

What are my responsibilities to the world if I am a follower of Jesus?

DISCUSS

Why is the body of Christ the best way to describe a Covenant community? What does this show us about what Covenant is really like?

What would it look like for us to grow in submission like Paul did?

What are some practical ways you could begin living out of the Covenant as an agent of the Kingdom?

Where is Jesus desperately needed in your community?

PLAN

What *kairos* has God brought to mind as you considered Covenant and Kingdom at work in the early church? How does God want you to respond to this *kairos*?

ACCOUNT

How will you record what God is leading you to do? How will you share your plan with someone else?

ACT

How did you follow through on your plan?

SECTION 12

Tools for Interpretation

COVENANT AND KINGDOM
CONCLUSION
PAGES 232–251

KEY QUOTES

Conclusion

The Bible is essentially about God, our loving Father, inviting us to know him in the most intimate of relationships. It is about discovering that this God whom we call "Daddy" is also the King of the universe, who calls us to represent him in the world. We will always wrestle with a sense of inadequacy when faced with this task, but this, surrendered into the hands of a loving Father, becomes the context through which his life and power flow. It is in weakness that God's power is made perfect.

page 251

OBSERVE One of the first questions to ask when you come to a passage of Scripture is whether it is primarily about Covenant or about Kingdom. Ask this question of your favorite Bible verse or Bible story. What does this tell you about your tendency toward Covenant or Kingdom?

REFLECT Which of the verses in the tools for interpretation found in chapter 17 stuck out most to you? Why do you think they resonated? How did they illuminate Covenant and/or Kingdom to you?

Think back on the whole of this guide. How would you describe Covenant differently today than when you started? How would you describe Kingdom differently today than when you started?

DISCUSS

Which do you feel more at home with—Covenant or Kingdom? Why?

How do you need to grow in Covenant? How do you need to grow in Kingdom?

PLAN

God is inviting you into Covenant relationship with him, and he wants to give you Kingdom responsibility. So ask yourself:

- Where do you sense God's invitation?
- Where do you sense God's challenge?
- Is anything holding you back?
- Who do you need to partner with?

Use these questions to make a plan to take what you've learned in this guide and actually include it as part of your everyday life.

ACCOUNT

How will you record what God is leading you to do? How will you share your plan with someone else?

ACT

How did you follow through on your plan over the short term and the long term?

www.ingramcontent.com/pod-product-compliance
Lightning Source LLC
Chambersburg PA
CBHW071240090426
42736CB00014B/3156

* 9 7 8 0 9 9 9 0 0 3 9 7 8 *